The Beautiful

Ximena Escobar

"At the heart of the poems lies a poignant exploration of love and loss, as Escobar grapples with the fragility of human connections and the pain of separation. Through her evocative imagery and lyrical prose, she invites readers to confront the bittersweet reality of saying goodbye and the enduring hope that love transcends even the deepest of sorrows.
A luminous testament to the power of poetry to illuminate the hidden corners of the soul."

-Hope Haugstad, book reviewer

If ever a secret was too beautiful not to share, it is Ximena Escobar's inaugural poetry collection, "The Secret Beautiful". Rich, yet nuanced; honest, yet inspired; alternately illuminating and enigmatic: these are poems about love, life and longing, that curl up in the lap of your imagination and purr.

-Shawn M. Klimek, poet & author

The Secret Beautiful. Some of her poems are lighter in nature, such as the ones that focus on themes like love, while others are darker and more graphic, especially those concerned with grief...They all encompass the very universal emotions that we experience as humans, and some of the phrasing is truly spectacular.
Reading this collection felt like diving into Escober's soul, and her ability to portray such intense emotions through her writing was admirable."

-Ashley Nestler, poet, author, bookstagrammer
IG: @peachykeenreviews, and @the_horror_maven

"Xiomena Escobar's words were at times haunting, at times intense, but always beautiful. The nautical theme that wove throughout the book wouldn't necessarily be my first choice if I were putting a collection together, but in this case, it worked quite well.
I will not be forgetting this collection anytime soon"

-Hannah Wolfram, book coach, & editor
TT & IG: @hmwolfram

To all who appear in these verses… You have become me.

Contents

Sea Glass

through the ripples above, the sun
shines like something attainable.
her cold heart envisions
a tangible sphere. she grasps it,
like a large pearl to wear of
everything she isn't. everything she wants to be.
She feels it, beat its mute
luminescence. calling for her
sea glass heart, unburied by a
flurry of sands. she can be
anything,
as long as the heart is surfaced.

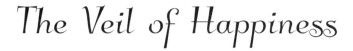

The Veil of Happiness

The water veiling her gaze was
home—not sadness—a sea of
transparency, a throne, a jewel.
the spark
of her madness, home in her darkness.
the glow
of a depth too far
is an aquarium cup of hands
infinite, as the whole universe, a sunken
star too distant, too alien to accept

that is where the heart is,
that is where she spins
behind the cloudy curtain of her tears.

No one saw her splashing in the puddles.
no one saw the mermaid
splashing in those ugly school shoes,

weighed down by the hem of her jeans,
making her late to the party

Sink,
in the glow of the place you came from,

The memory of happiness,
The veil of Happiness.

....

The Heart of the Ocean

ruby lips to hide behind.
pearls, to match my scales.
I swim unseen
in my hazy universe,
blinking fireflies
at the bottom of the pool.
emerald green
glass walls, find my palms,
but it is my own grip
around the gem,
like an amulet to save me—
I'll be the last to laugh

I am the jewel
within the jewel
that only I know
that I carry

The Secret Beautiful

to swim in the centre of wholeness,
wrapped by being,
hugged by deafness,
to be
the secret beautiful,
the secret wonderful

one day you will find me,
one day I will shoot up to the sky where smiles
aren't blades,
I will shine in those eyes,
moist
opened
slapped, by the treasure
they discover
me,

my beauty,
untamed,
my mermaid hair streaming,

screaming,

I exist.

....

Icicle Nearness

Icicle nearness,
Deliciously dangerous
Cold edge of whispers

Black Water

Closing my eyes upon your nearness
I submerged in your darkness,
I soared on the wavelets,
flowed entwined with you, through the water
Spiralling in the warmth of your kiss
I surfaced
with a gush, under the firmament
Spread with angel arms floating
on crystalline ripples, shining in the darkness

And I saw our future in the sky's story
for I failed to read the black
in between each beautiful star,
a cruel waterfall was waiting
and I plummeted into the abysmal cold,
I sank in the ocean of ink
at the other side of your pen,
As black water leaked from
my perforated soul,

I crumpled up your note
I tossed it
in a black pool of
starlessness

....

Ocean of G&T

I still hear you
talking through the soda water,
black and silver
ocean of self;
I sang my heart out,
In the fire-orange room.

it's like trying to catch bubbles,
looking for
the *me* in your eyes,
so says the mirror
implanted in the ocean bed;
eye tunnels,
my reflection

my skull, my gut,
my fish tale, my fairytale—
I fall into
the rusty drain;
the white porcelain sink
has cracked, a hair-thin thread
your murmur,
dissipates

Don't look down on me.
Pull me
from these black hole eyes.
Kiss my dripping lips.
Love my fears away.

....

I Will Love You

I close my eyes to the redness,
listen to the fire crackle,
lose all sense of my surroundings,
except
for the hug
all-surrounding
of its closeness.
your memory, like the fire,
spits with his nearing steps.
I open my eyes
to orange reflections,
his eyes sparkle

like yours used to sparkle.
I sip his wine,
swallow my longing for you.
Today marks the beginning of a new love,
but the flames, darling,
will always be ours.

As long as fire burns,
I will love you.

....

A Moment

a moment slowed
by nearness, paused
by breath, lengthened
by pulse
a moment frozen
by breeze, blessed
by shine, stretched
by sky
A moment lifted
by veils, raised
by spirits, blurred
by wine
Words combined
like liquid amber,
slowly passing
through every curve,
of glass hour,
every coil,
of throat
that each is caressed,

a moment stressed
by eyeliner
reddened by pain,
swallowed by song,
a moment, wrapped
by grief, lifted
by resolve,
as bare feet stand on polished daylight
spread like tomorrow on the floorshine,
a moment elevated
by wind, combed
by guitar chords
I share it with you

A moment, any moment
lifted
so high I
plunge
into the shallows
of a moment
gone.

Hug Knows

I know we love each other.
It's all in the hug.
squeezed in a casual
oblivious, hello.
in that extra time spent,
touching base
saying,
what we can't with words.
If only for a second,
half a second, our cheeks linger
staying, *stretching* the pain
lest we forget it.

In and out of
gates,
of doors, in transit
our unattended baggage
is seen to
for the briefest second
in a hug.
until we scar like landscape,
streambeds
ever divergent.

....

Not in vain, the river flows
our body knows
to age,
let the children
absorb in the banks
as scattered wishes
seeding colourful memories.

Love is as simple
as hungry,
as tired,
love is as simple
as that which gets lost
like a piece of Lego
fucking hurts,
it's there or it isn't,
look for it until you find it
or leave it, leave it,
you don't want the thing anymore,
whatever we built, we don't want it,
hoover it up into the vacuum
of indifference,
under the rug
there is nothing left
but a hug

....

the warmth
of your seat,
the side you slept on,
the smile that opens naturally
upon a memory
when you, only you will do
to tread upon those leaves with,
crossing the rain or shine through the trees
silent,
separate together.

the hug knows
the sinking in our tongues.
overboard, tossed
love.

Separate Together

It's funny thinking that all along
we were looking at the same horizon
all those times I ran from the waves
you were in the same ocean,
splashing, laughing,
only at the other side,
that every time
I lived, convinced,
that I was destined to be alone,
you were always there
and that one day
thrown astray like dice on the game board
we'd land on the same flight
flying over that same old sea
looking down from opposite windows,
having similar thoughts, perhaps
sitting by opposite wings
until we saw each other,
through the ladies between us
(I guess they were only as old as we are now)
through all that time,
all that distance,
right there above the water…
and that's all the horizon we wanted.

Surfaced

My rib encircled
by warm-blooded
ethereal palms
I bear the flow
of my uncertain breath,
gripping the bone
dangling in my carcass
I'm a loose kite lifted
by your wilful bluster,

thrust by a leaf vein
cast into the blue
expanse
between the cage bars
I once again forget
the angst of a pause,
distracted by shapes
of clouds in your eyes,
pulled
by your balloon lungs
surfaced

back into the circle
of your arms.

Inadequate

parched pores
drenched in thirst
open
paper mouths
drinking
your evaporated essence.
it's draining
feeling you
trickle out of my veins
like tiny droplets
in much larger tubes,
an unfit lover
or an empty pen,
leaving but a watermark imprint
of you.
or is it me?
the weightlessness
so inadequate,
leaves your shoes unfilled,
or does it mine?
stares back at me
from this infertile
prayer.

....

Thoughts of Anne

Anne scans the emptiness,
searching for a sign of life;
a rustle, a glimmer, a flurry
anything
as the echo of a prayer bounces
in her mind,
but no voice stirs the leaves,
no beauty
reverberates her heart.
only the wind
before the blade;
only the wind.

....

Eve

Eve swallowed
Adam's apple
fluttering plastered eyelashes;
rainbows cast
by morning dew teardrops,
even when it is
ever so late,
even when still
Eve waits for the sun to sink

Ruby slippers
glitter better in the darkness,
high heels sparkling
high
in the inverted cone of stage light;
standing on her toes
she's an arrow through the disco ball,
beautiful axis
right in the centre of a spinning world

....

She casts square mirrors
stabbing our eyes like a car crash,
every shape is queer inside
each little square,
amorphous in the rigidity
of straight lines and angles,
bleeding the makeup off our faces,
alluvium of fragments
washing us clean

She's ever more beautiful,
lying in her stripy lounge pants,
under the weight of the dog
but she is
and always will be
a star,

all the more visible
in the darkness.

Guernica

Her body's still hanging from a gate like a bag,
except the bag is around her head
and a loop around the neck still dents the skin
gravity,
still breaks the neck bone,
purple blueprints
where gloves were worn,
she always was a splash of colour,
twisting her balloons,
blowing her little bubbles,
watching them rise and shine,
swell and burst
like illusions.
Look at her
collecting all the eyes,
splattered on the tarmac
they saw everything;
they saw the black souls
treading their tank trail,
like beautiful lace, trimming the battlefield

....

Branch and metal, petal and flag,
they saw the dandelions
break through the concrete,
they saw her splattered teardrop,
multiplying all the mirrors,
the giant canvas
portraying for eternity
the beautiful stillness
of this chaos,

How we love the shock
how we love the silence,
inseparable from our own time,
the beauty of our fathers' pain

In each other's eyes.

Taxi Ride

where are they now;
those who tortured and murdered us—
gone,
like ants in the gravel,
driving our taxis,
mopping our hallways.
hidden as always, in their sameness.
hidden in their plaid and paisley.
hidden in their denim.
once they bore their boots and arms,
they carved our souls with their footprints,
pierced our hearts with their gunshots,
tattooed us with their bruises,
punished us for our fashion.
who hides behind those covered eyes,
sunshades, in the rear-view mirror
they're everywhere, the mirror skyscrapers,
showing us the brightest reflection
of our blindness.

....

Doll

doll
never got to see
the tallest building,
the highest wheel,
the queen
waving the fortune
promised by a lucky hand.
doll,
didn't get to shake
the lucky hand of success,
the city lights
she came from.

I'd wished for her pretty
(blue eyes like the sky
gold hair like the sun).
I'd wished for the Alice band,
the dress.
never occurred to me
plastic
never hears explosions;
never occurred to me,
a sealed mouth never
tastes steel.

it's not our fault
we look to some
like undeserved happiness.
stolen happiness
in a box
wrapped in ribbons

she still looks pretty in the debris,
on the cover of every newspaper,
she's bearable to look at.
funny,
never ever
never have I ever
wanted to grow up.
never occurred to me,
someday I'd give anything.

my lucky hand too.

The Last of Justin

Impregnated
By awful certainty
Seeding a moment's eternity
You linger
In the centuries-old water
Eyelids weighing
On ocean blue irises
Frozen to the daylight
Of multicoloured dreams.
Like aqueous tendrils,
You stretch through the membrane
Mysterious curtain
Separating two worlds.
The immeasurable reach
Of your absence
Means
You are also sky.
Tinted waves
Blue, purple, yellow,
Break in the forever sunset
Of my grief for you.

Kali's Mandala

a collection of images
with no coherent meaning
spun, kaleidoscopic
pulled itself together
in a sunflower eye,
a poem aligned with the centre of chaos
flowering an explosion
of multiple…

darkness
is also a colour,
seeping beads spilled their stain,
as Kali's mandala broke your destiny.

winking with her terrible eye,
cracked in the middle by the darkest rivulet,
caused by the careless bouncing
of a young goddess skipping,
tripping on her second set of arms,
falling on a broken beer bottle,
cutting through vein.

her eyelashes flutter
pretty reflections on the green glass,
loose beads on the pavement
twinkling,
decorate the darkness
like spinning galaxies.

you still look beautiful
in her dreadful universe,
even now
you still look colourful,
even now
you warm the heart
in death, as you did in heaven,

watch you jump from star to star
before the rain blurs all the shapes
before we drown in sinking mud
before we pause, consider, think, remember.
see the beauty
of her black tears
leaving
sluggish rainbows on the pavement,
see the spill of broken dreams,
see the mud, the colours
through a water universe.

in the pulp of destruction
all that is left is creation,
broken fragments,
bleeding palm lines
dripping, Pollockian landscapes.
weeping, as I am,
on your empty canvas.

Silence

Silence finds me,
or do I find Silence,
it's me who steps out
through a curtain of transparency
and seeks her,
where the wind is blowing,
where peace lies like the surface of stillness,
my tranquil cup with all its landscape
whispers,
I contain mountains.
But time always comes
when time is over,
a gust of train-wind forces us to turn,
here,
is where I want to stay,

....

47

I fall in the sand-slide.

step

into the thunderous rattle of silence

raping me, stake of coolness shaking

cracking, breaking, it opens me

so she can bounce inside me and shake me

sore,

is my voice erupting in scream.

Birthed, by the concave end of a moment

I roll

on the concrete edge of a platform

breathe,

enough

is enough.

Jake

your chest is all I think of
when I think surrender,
on sand
      I fall
            like sunshine
                  to rest

I land on you
sleep on you
burn on you,

salt of the earth
is you.

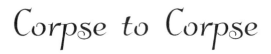

Corpse to Corpse

I can't run.
I can't run to the sea
and drown myself.
I can just breathe,
breathe as I lie here,
grasp the lose-earth-strength,
pull myself, damn it,
drag my broken legs,
dream of my nose in the water.
Eyelids pricked with unbearable sight
bite the enclosure of eternal abandon;
for death to birth me is my eternal prayer,
that I will soon have earned my dissolution.
Shed this coat of pain and flesh;
left behind all the sand trails.
Gone they are.
like clusters of raindrops,
dissipating
in the fog of
this tired grey brain.

....

Drizzled upon me by each wave
my heart leaps like a blown-up soldier.
Damn it, the sound,
of a million cries drowning
at each pull of my helpless hands,
crawling, deserting to the water.
They float like sacks of bones in the tide
hitting the rocks
like my clavicle, the birth canal.
Dreaming the edge of time,
cascading
in the amniotic sea foam,
breaking on the desert
of corpse to corpse.

Gripping wet grains
of standing time,
this earth is my mother
and my grave.

Only the Words

clinging to time
with saltwater claws
with foam, with breath
on my windowpane,

only the words
will do.

....

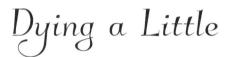

Dying a Little

Dying a little
is the watercolour stone
chalking my palm,
the beauty of grey
weighing on my heart like mud

Your eyes of wonder sinking, but
smiling, through the daffodils
like when the yellow sun breaks the cloud
and you wonder, perhaps you're in heaven

Dying a little is the gravestones,
dying a little is the child
footprint between the grass blades
stories,
weighing on my heart like mud,

Dying a little is breaking your heart
dying a little is ripping you away,
soiling my hands with your flagellum roots
of nerve ends aching,
reaching for fingertips
as the horizon stretches,

Will you love me? is dying a little
handprint fading,
shapes diluting,
in the watercolour grey
outside the lines.

When the Time Comes

dampness,

later.

like I didn't take off the wet clothes.

that is what you do to me.

weight of breathless

morning dew,

there's no pulling off this cloak.

there's no pulling off these socks.

the chill

of your steps,

lurking

on the soft ground.

I breathe you in the muddy air.

nearness of earth is your breath

fogging

the dimness of a cool sun.

intimate as flesh is your distance,

cruel, blade-cold

irony,

shackles me with iron fists.

there's no need to impose yourself upon me like this,

I have, always, been entirely yours.

deep in the innermost darkness
the door was always ajar for you.
never was there a key within our reach,
never a glint with which to lock away the unknown.
keep your sparkle
from seeing
the immaterial marrow
of our essence.

I'm cold inside only by your shadow
until you strip me of the womb of my flesh
and starless eternity puts out the cold like a fire blanket,
you'll evaporate with me,
bitter sea mist,
fizzing my hair, my wool, my soul.

ailing, I'll go on,
gum boots treading on the wet grass.
febrile eyes still seeking solace
in a distant
pale-yellow star.

the notion of begging you
to hold me with a beating heart,

when the time comes.

....

Raven is the Colour of Your Soul

Raven is the colour of your soul
for I can only perceive you in the darkness
Feel you restless
Bear your prison
Swallow my hourglass vein
Pulse
to the beat
of your silent anxiousness

wings flapping
stir
the muteness
opening black eyes
to your avian wind
I'm thrust to the shallow ground
of light beyond a million fractures,
broken barriers, releasing you

And I sigh, in a flurry of blackbirds
beautiful stone angel,
dressed in moss,
wrapped by the swift
spiral of a dream
you wear your ruin,

as a crystal raindrop
settles in your tear duct
see the birds within it,
before an earthquake reveals your hollowness.

Fluttering
Within these corners
I breathe to the rhythm
Of your despair.

58

Don't Wait

In the underwater interior
of a luminous ancient ruin
I breathe a turquoise sky
akin to the space
where words blossom unspoken
waiting for a blow
to ripple the stagnant hollow in my lips
but time won't wait for this poem,
death won't wait,
for the flurrying of sands
in these inflated lungs,
the stirring of the hourglass
will not wait for will,

.·········.

time will not wait
for a perfect dune to settle,
for an elongated tear
to part in the back of the throat,
children
will not wait for you
to swallow
any realisation,

the propitious light
to close one's eyes in completeness,
before a final darkness
drains the skull of all the beauty,
will not wait.

....

Pour Me

Pour me on
the blank page
spill me
on this empty sky
seed me on a bed
of verses
rain on
my longing for you

Here lies,
carved
on the headboard
my eternal devotion.

....

Joy

A gust of wind and
a pencil rolled onto the floor,
that's when their eyes met,
that's when fingers brushed under the desk
and later, she wrote his name on the back of her hand
and later, his hand lowered slowly upon her knee
but the moment, in a breeze, was always gone
like goosebumps,
saved by the bell,
missed by the bottle,
a broken clock,
a minute hand too slow.
But a favourable gust,
it spun the weathervane,
her dress ballooned,
he coveted
to know all her secrets,
he coveted
being the wind
slipping between her folds,
he coveted
to raise her, make her soar
in her dress of petals
like wishes.

She saw herself spinning in the sky of his eyes,
when he rang the doorbell and a rush of wind
blew his tie onto his face,
windchimes swayed like wedding bells
clinking like wineglasses
spilling Joy
running down the golden fields of summer,
the flash at the end of a magic spell,
gone
in a moment
But even if the minute hand, too quickly
squeezes the wick between its fingertips,
Joy
still looks like honey and sunshine in their eyes,
helping old mum and dad out of the car,
sagging like candle wax

as life, in a breeze, is gone already
whisking the leaves on their tombstone,
engraved,
no wind can ever erase them.

Girl Disappearing

sprouting in
the flutter of eyelids
blossom, imperceptible
wind of butterflies,
under the covers
under the t-shirt,
girl disappearing

in woman.

....

Black Rose

deep in the silence at the end of days
when the boys sleep, but I cannot,
I feel the crack stretch through my body,
your seed opening like a clam
cracks me like dry earth,
the seed you are, breaking,
giving birth in the cool moist soil,
shooting a vine through the unknown hour
breaks me,
and makes you.

and I search with fingertips,
soil under my nails,
feel in the damp earth
blind,
I cannot grasp you
are the path
you've traced without me,

beautiful snake
licking the night
with black velvet petals...
I can at least
be in awe of you.

....

Little Earthquake

she lies on the bedcover
hair
spread like an octopus,
orange as fire,
she lies
open
like a mollusc
on the bedcover.
a goddess splitting
like paint about to crack,
for all the world to see
what lies ahead of destruction,
what lies beneath
temporal truths.

she lies amorphous
stretching finger-like projections,
reaching for starfishes
they land on her, suck on her.
until she is no more *her*
and becomes entirely something else.
a fire burning in those eyes,
tamed
by vintage-blue irises.

they hide an unmade dragon.
she doesn't know it at this point
but under this semblance of youth
and shabby chic venetian church dome colours
she always was an old soul.
but this
this
one could have never expected.
there really is a dragon in there
and this perhaps explains the pride
of only one who can lie open like this.
a man's pride—
plucking grass blades
instead of leg hair.

of course, I missed the whole thing.
next I looked she was already broken
into a million pieces—pulverised.
blossomed in the darkness
like all the magic in the world.
she'd shattered like a fucking earthquake,
and all I can do now is walk on the plaster,
see through the ruin,
the flame,

....

for she has already eclipsed the sun,
looking down on me from slit pupils
mirroring,
the cut of her absence.
flames mirroring
the ethereal tentacles
like goddess hair strands
wrapped around my grateful arms.

it burns,
how much I miss her.

....

The Bond

to be a string.
after all the muscle.
all the earth
to topple all the scales,
have you slide, plummet
into my embrace.
for a bond to be
all that is left,
a loose tie thrown
like a shoelace
under your sneaker.
after all those years
to be but
a thread in your history,
the shadow
of an old cross
above the headboard...

all I want is the reality,
all I want is to
scrape the crusty sugar
on the commissure of your kisses,
for that,
I can believe

....

Bare Walls

I curl back into hiding
in that hole that shame forced me out of
so I could live
the coveted years
I wasted
creating bonds
to someday unhang
from those nails right there—
family photos,
ribbons—
strangle myself with them—
whip my hands to convince myself
I deserve the loss
I've already begun to suffer.
bending like a burning fingernail,
tossed, flicked to the outskirts
I curl,
cradled in the memory of mother's love.
sleeping,
dreaming in that bud
I pray,

no one will notice my bare walls.
I pray
I am wrong.
I pray

I am just having a bad day.

....

Behind the Hood

you don't have to hide, darling.
I'm only unhanging your wings
from under the coats,
the sports bag, my umbrella,
I'm sorry I let them gather dust.
look how much they have grown!
look how much they have grown
in the shade.
the black and white television set,
always unplugged. lit by daylight,
lit by sprinklers,
it's like that with you.
the girl you were,
is running in your unlit eyes,
I know it,
even if I don't see you behind the hood.
she only had to outstretch
her little arms, remember?
lifting us both to the climax of wonderment.
see her now
sail
the honey rivers of your hair
spilling down your shoulders,
even if I cannot see your face
behind the hood.

your glitter nails, pressing the phone screen,
cast electronic lights in your eyes.
even if I cannot see
the marks under your sleeves.
even if I don't see anything,
I see your wings
look at them,
heavy as winter.
heavy as all the water under the bridge.
like a feathered seal
they writhe in my arms,
pulling away from me
as though I have hurt you.

a cigarette burn
opens a Botticelli sky.
and I
fix my eyes upon storm clouds
weeping rainbows
watching you rise again.

kneeling on a carpet of feathers
I know I shall never remove
the hairs from your hairbrush
I'll never
throw away your baby-teeth
but I will
dust this pain away,
watch the spill
like fall through the ceiling hole,

candyfloss bruises
snowing like cotton balls,
even when I cannot see your face
behind the hood.

Tired

I want to be tired,
and make you tired.
rest together and breathe
a little.
how I long to lie
as only a mother can.
rest,
my heart under your ear,
be the earth and heal,
seal, without a tantrum
only the privilege
of giving
a little
love:

a warm crater
just your size,
to sleep in.

....

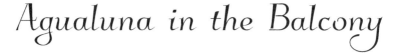

Agualuna in the Balcony

Agualuna in the balcony
leans over the handrail
lifting little heels
creasing
patent leather shoes.
if I could climb down,
twirl myself
around
plaited jelly snakes.
but she'd rather be Alice
in the burrow of daddy's hugs
squeezing her lungs
constricting her.
if air could be
clear water rising,
like when tears well up,
I'd skydive through the waves.
I'd swim underwater
I'd hear the whale singing
swaying,
like when daddy carried me,

....

gentle teeth pulling me
down

     down

         down
by the frill of my sock
It only wants to play,
but my heart beats like men marching,
and the whale worries.
It shoots up to save me,
so fast that when she breaks through the surface,
I project through my own mouth,
I skyrocket out of my own mouth like a shooting star
and never look down

when the dandelion puff blows
against the asphalt

....

76

Violeta y el Mar

She didn't understand his coldness.
She didn't understand his restless murmur
of here and away.
She didn't understand the cloud of his heart
Buried secrets she felt in her own bones
Cells stirring,
Waiting.
She longed for his depth.
Overwhelming reflection of the sky.
Her smallness longed to disappear
in the immensity
of his strength.

He pushed her away
He warned her with fury,
But
By then she had decided
She was nothing without him.
He got in the way of
Every conversation
Every poem
Every blank canvas
Until,
Her bones became
one of his secrets.

....

Mother

immense those mountains,
like time exposed. beautiful wound
reminding us of who we are.
dividing me between
my life and yours,
the girl and now.

if I don't look
if I don't see them,
the ungraspable beginning
set like beautiful clouds in the valley.
the old days,
they are always there,
that feeling of being loved,
you,
underneath everything
bears my soul.

my soles
set on the certainty of loving you,
on my path without you
I love to love you,
in the absence of my presence

know
that I am always there,

like those mountains.

. . . .

Metamorphosis

you lie, a bundle,
wrapped in eggshell wings.
the dirty white stillness of aluminium blinds
lets in gold threads of dream.
vent to a vacant yet luminous universe,
a vacuum like the murmur of recycled air,
for a moment, I feel we are both flying,
that air-conditioned aeroplane feeling,
trickles flowing,
crystal fluid running like blood,
a rain stick in my ear.
you have already left
in the current within.
you have already emptied
plastic veins.

flowers have the habit of blossoming unseen.
gold dust lifts, cast by your movement.
a luminous mountain,
a monolith, you are risen,
as shine breaks through the horizontal slits
illuminating moth wings
open, like pirate sails.

Treading on
the shattered chrysalis.
I follow you,
chasing but a flame in the sky,
squinting upon the radiant emptiness,

hooked by fragments,
to our unbearable lightness.

....

Aqua Irises

Your aqua irises jitter
suffering the nascent outburst
desperate to gush out of our throats.
I see it snake in your neck-veins,
twitching, flapping;
I don't want you to ever eject your love for us.
But a barrel resonates,
the same white muteness
and colour of my mind, this white
surgical space, this purgatory—
I scream with you,
gag
on the wings you are retching,
your skeletal jaw wide open,
bearing the powder cloud
ejaculated,
the dove that flies away

....

I stretch my fingers tensely on the screen,
colourless and odourless
as the liquid flowing through the pipes inside me—
I feel them with an uncomfortable numbness
as though my body is waking
attached to some kind of machine,
but that is a movie I once saw, yes,
slipping in through the air conditioning,
or whatever those vents are in the halls,
just above the white tile floors—
sterile dermis
I inhabit

I dream the window open, darling,
should you care to find me.

I'm not sure your index would even slow as it would scroll past me,
down the whitest plasma such as I conceive of here,
beating instead for a gap of blue
between the lines,
that smell of grass we cannot grasp,
not even brush with calloused fingertips.
They've forgotten the steel guitar strings, the wine inside our
mouths.

,.........

Those are not the shapes keeping you alive, already,
not our song, anymore
but the tweeting of birds,
the threads of sunshine through the leaves.
Crystalline rivulets we only ever dreamed of;
we only borrowed them from storybooks
yet, you miss them, like you lost them.
I guess, like an orphan who never knew his mother.

Look at you.
Look at you tread on the dead birds.
I won't suffer your bones,
I will only suffer the painlessness,
gripping the air separating us.
Gripping the air between our locked eyes,
as the same boat cracks,
but it wasn't the same boat.
You and I afraid of the darkness;
I was only afraid of solitude.

.........,

Following the amoeba shape
escaping
infinitely
you,
time and time again,
diagonally away
and taking off again
forever.
Light was not a mere purple stain,
we never could perceive the darkness
absolutely.
Here, in the certainty of light
I'll cling to your imprint lest your eyes fade,
cling to the scar where,
like a watermark,
we remain.

Spiral

There must exist
A certain combination of words
Uttered in the right order
Poured in the right quantities
Into the swirl at the end of my spoon
There must exist
The perfect potion
The perfect mixture
To make you love me

....

The Bridge

A growing distance,
a changing landscape,
I no longer see
the bridge we used to meet upon.
I no longer care for
your watercolour imprint,
dangling dream catcher
sweeping on my shoulder,

feather duster faerie
lifts pollen butterflies,
seedlings on new meadows.
I skip to newfound melodies,
to stumble on the rock of you
for the duration of beautiful light...

the painlessness of us is,
you have become me,

our story is but light and air
in these words.

Alone With You

edge of ease,
beginning of self,
verses and mirrors
swaying
in my wine glass.
I told you of explosions,
I dreamt of meteors,
death would come crashing
like the promise of the waves.
I knew it would fall short,
I knew you didn't get it,
when I told you,
and you weren't afraid.
A million stars,
are still
in your eyes,
the glow of their melancholy,
is my company.

The Window

Little birds
in the sun rays,
paintbrush sinking
into the chrome
yellow, feel of
your presence;
liquid silk is
luminous and cold,

I drift into the stillness
of cracked paint on the windowsill.
There's not a breeze
to breathe
into the skeletal trees.
The impenetrable forest
of thorns, in my lungs
whistles,
are you dying?

I lie
wheezing
on a down-feather pillow
dreaming birdsong,
dreaming
summer in my windowpane,
silver rings
tossed in the soap dish:
opal,
moonstone.

Must there always
be shadow when the sun shines?
Must grandmother's hand
always
be cold?
Must I
always
cling to life
desperately?

Somewhere

somewhere
on the edge of a completion
I anticipate your breath
like grass expects the air,
your wind shapes me
in your image and likeness,
see the Irish sea cliffs
stand your enormity

the expanse of my interior,
blended into otherness
to bear you like land bears,
without resistance

....

Sink

Sink your absence
in a sea of forgetfulness
Sink my hurt of your silence
Sink the scream of my frustration
Swallowed
in relentless coldness
Sink my humiliation
of loving you still
in the nauseating restlessness
of losing you.

....

Invisible

The girl next door
She is a visible woman
She is the woman I wanted to be
Back when I was visible,
A different book
Every second day
Sitting on her front porch
She reads the day away,
My dog stops to smell the roses
And not once she lifts her face
She's sensed this silhouette before
of no one she would want to know,

She sees no shapes
in the cotton cloud sky,
no dolphin nor tiger,
no self-portrait
in this passerby.

Back when I was visible,
She would have raised her chin
Forged a half smile,
Something about the weather,
We would have had a glass together,

But there is freedom in being invisible,
Waiting beyond the corner of her eye,
Waiting for the puppy to pee,
I tell myself, I could get used to this.
It's liberating,
watching a silly movie on the plane
Shamelessly.

....

Perspective

I plunge
surrendered
to the blow
of rock bottom

Soundless explosion
of fractured
memories

Too minute
to put together,
too distant
infinitesimal stars

When the sky is south,
falling I am rising

surrendered to the blow
of hard-rock heights.

The Speculative Universe

The random universe gave me a tailbone.
I grew a fish tail
dressed it in sequins.
The random universe
spelled nothing's forever.
Scales should fall
from moonbeam branches.
A constellation of stars
float on the tide,
the beauty of everything lost
reflected in the sky.
Standing on footprints
I stare at the random arrangement
of this fantasy.
Pinned to gravity
I don't shed my tail.

....

Shining in the Water

no one said to look in the water for happiness
but lifting my heels off the edge of the rock
I jumped in coldness
like the saddest ending
of the most beautiful children's story,
fizzing up in bubbles and foam.

I like to think of blue-green scales
wrapping my shape and soul with warmth.
I like to think this is the destiny
and origin
of all sirens.
if you look carefully,
you can see them too
swimming within aqueous sunbeams.
this is where they bear
the light of dead galaxies,
the scrutiny
of alien eyes.

I never looked so beautiful,
shining in the water.

....

These Stories

These stories are breathing
the volume of excess,
rescued from the weightlessness
of spilled time
breathing, the loss of
wind
between the pages,
insects
smeared
like skid marks
by our fingerprints.

With any luck we look at
the same pinned butterflies,
the same beautiful beauty,
before we fan the book
with any luck we hold,
each other's hands on deck,
we're all on the same damned boat,
gazes aligned
in the horizon of our fear.

With any luck
we see each other before we die
and take all the stories

with us

Acknowledgements

The titles below have been previously published, some in different versions, or under different titles.

originally appeared on *Spillwords*, 2019-2022

"Mother"
"Doll"
"Hug Knows"
"Black Water"
"The Secret Beautiful"
"The Veil of Happiness"
"Silence" (as "Enough")
"Tired"
"Dying a Little"
"Kali's Mandala"

originally appeared in *Poetica, Vol. 1*, 2019

"Joy" (as "Winds of Love")

originally appeared in *Organic Ink, Vol. 1*, 2019
(out of print)

"Agualuna in the Balcony"
"Girl Disappearing"

originally appeared in *Sea Glass Hearts, 2*019

"Alone With You" (as "Conversations By the Sea")
"Jake" (as "Remembrance")
"Sink" (as "Wave of Regret")
"Violeta y el Mar" (as "Violet Returns")

originally appeared on *Melbourne Culture Corner*, Issue #7, 2021

"Aqua Irises"

....

originally appeared in *Paranormal Romance #3: Lockdown*, 2020

"I Will Love You"

originally appeared in *Eldritch & Ether*, 2022

"The Speculative Universe"
"When the Time Comes"

originally appeared in *Evermore 2*, 2023

"Raven is the Colour of Your Soul"

....

About the Author

XIMENA ESCOBAR has always held a deep-rooted affection for the art of writing. From letters to essays and lyrical compositions, she has explored a diverse range of genres. An adept player of Exquisite Corpse with her dearest friend, her creative wanderings led to several screenwriting projects. Though those didn't work out, she did have the opportunity to translate a musical in 2009.

A literary group on social media caught Ximena's attention in 2017, encouraging her to not only write more, but to begin submitting her short stories, poems, and micro-fiction. Her work has been published in over 50 anthologies by various indie publishers in Australia, America, and the UK. *The Secret Beautiful* is her debut solo title.

Ximena feels at home in three different countries. Born and raised in Chile, she now lives in Sydney with her husband, three children and Bobbi the dog.

Follow her on Instagram and Facebook.

Instagram: @these_stories_are_breathing
Facebook: @ximenautora

....

....

About the Publisher

THE RAVENS QUOTH PRESS is a boutique publisher based in Australia, dedicated to showcasing the best of international poetry craft in beautifully presented publications.

Follow us: **linktr.ee/TheRavensQuothPress**

Printed in the USA
CPSIA information can be obtained
at www.ICGtesting.com
JSHW021915140524
63135JS00003B/7

9 780975 667200